Returning to Nothingness

Songs of Contemplation

Rev. Luis Caldeira

ISBN-10: 061567951X
ISBN-13: 9780615679518

Dedication

This book was written for You

Acknowledgements

"A single sunbeam is enough to drive away any shadows."

—ST. FRANCIS OF ASSISI

My truth is that my breath rises and falls in the spirituality of imperfection.

Recently when asked what kind of Reverend I was, I could simply smile and humbly answer, "The real kind, just human, for I'm a great sinner trudging into God's heart."

This selection of songs that I share with you reveals just that, that like me, you, us, our humanness is what's makes us holy, for He is holy, and in His image He created us.

In gratitude I want to voice my thanks to Bill W., Dr.Bob, and Jimmy K., for they have offered me a design for living that made these pages possible.

To my dear Erik Pedersen, I love you my good man.

Almar Sator, my guardian angel, thank you.

To my dear friends Randy Davila, and Dr. Kathleen Hudson, my deepest appreciation for who you are.

I also want to offer my thankfulness to my dear Holly Weseloh, a true friend, even (especially) when my waters are troubled, you always have a way of calming the tides.

And to the men of Saint Francis of Assisi Recovery House, I Love You Kiddos.

To my Loving Mystical Christ,

I'm Yours, Sweet Creator, I'm Yours.

Luis Caldeira

Foreword

"Out beyond ideas of wrongdoing and rightdoing, there is a field. I'll meet you there. When the soul lies down in that grass, the world is too full to talk about. Ideas, language, even the phrase *each other* doesn't make any sense."

—RUMI (TRANSLATED BY COLEMAN BARKS)

Many authors in the spiritual genre offer heavy handed guidance to readers as they walk the spiritual path, instructing them on how to think, what to do, and when to act.

My friend, author Rev. Luis Caldeira, is not to be included in that group.

With a style reminiscent of the poetic master Jalāl ad-Dīn Muḥammad Rūmī, Luis's words require a requisite amount of reflection and fermentation to ascertain their deeper meaning.

Rather than take you by the hand and lead you down the path of right and wrong, Luis challenges you to forge your own way, and offers thought provoking (and more importantly, thought ceasing) direction for your journey.

This is not a book to be read in one sitting, or even two. But rather, these words are to be savored. I encourage you to treat this work like a book of daily meditations, and to read a passage with the aim of contemplating its inner essence. The answers you seek will arise from the stillness, and guide you on your *Return to Nothingness.*

Randy Davila

July 2012

A Word From The Editor

"Ring the bells that still can ring

Forget your perfect offering

There is a crack in everything

That's how the light gets in."

Leonard Cohen's "Anthem"

Upon completion of the work with Rev. Luis Caldeira, I found myself integrating the prayers and poems into my own breathing.

I did not "edit" or "translate," rather I entered a process of creation with him, asking him about meaning and words, and breathing with him. What a valuable experience for me, and I know readers will also have an "experience": of the prayers as well as of the poetry.

Delight was part of the process for me as Luis often looked at the poem in wonder, "Who wrote that?" We both knew that the words came through him not from him.

This collection contains autobiography as he bravely uses his own life as fuel in the creative process. But more than a life story, this collection invites the reader to breathe with Luis and see what arises in the heart and spirit.

Love songs from the spirit? Perhaps. Guides to internal journeys? Perhaps. I know for me the experience was life-changing. Enjoy.

Kathleen Hudson, Ph.D.

July 2012

Returning
to
Nothingness

Songs of Contemplation

Rev. Luis Caldeira

❀ WELCOME HOME ❀

Have you eaten the bread that the devil as has kneaded?

Have you washed your soul in the waters of sin?

Have you drunk from the cup of sorrows?

And forgotten your blessings within?

Run for the hurt?

Created hurricanes?

Cursed the beggar that fed you?

And begged the carpenter to turn your water into wine?

Well....

Welcome home sweet brother

Welcome home...

For the rock becomes a diamond.

Just like you, a precious stone.

Climb the pit into the sunlight.

Grasp this tired hand of mine.

You are not alone,

Welcome home.

Welcome home.

Welcome home.

❋ THE PATH ❋

Have you been invited to the path?

Did you stumble upon it?

Or was your sacrifice and offering your motivation for the journey?

Many blind men have greater vision than the one who has sight,

And trudging onward is but an invisible choice, like sensing the wind.

If the ant is as great as the elephant,

And the sunrise, sunset sister,

Can sorrow be embraced as the joys of life are embraced?

What other opportunities are there?

For the path is what is,

And the journey unfolds with, or without one's permission.

❋ WELCOMING THE UNWELCOMED ❋

Welcome unwanted, unwelcomed one,

Sit; please sit in my temple of transformation,

As my body rests in your coals of ice and your rains of fire, I welcome you,

That's right my dear one,

We are no strangers to one another,

Forging the metal of time,

Shaping the rock into a gem,

What a great teacher you have been and remain.

Welcome again unwanted, unwelcomed one,

Amuse me with your element of surprise when the curtains of my soul are drawn into the fake safety of life,

You slap me merciless and laugh at me,

I must respect you for your cleverness,

And there's also the flowing serenity of soul, ever so assuring of the divine within,

You punch me in the belly violently and roar senselessly,

I must bow to your subtleness,

For I know you my dear,

Yes, I know you.

Your angel wings disguised as bitterness,

Your light as foul loneliness,

Your healing, desperation,

And so it is that you unveil my way to the Beloved,

And again, again we become one.

And yes, I bow, to you, I bow.

❀ Silence ❀

Run into the silence and hear the voice of truth,

Call upon the stillness and be moved by the waves of presence,

Claim unknowing and drink the unspoken wisdom of ages,

Walk in quiet purpose and be blessed without measure,

A drop in the ocean is but a simple drop, yet, becomes it, the ocean nevertheless, and it belongs, it belongs...

❀ SEASONS ❀

Meet me with the hope of spring,

Meet me at the gates of light,

Seeking the One that guides us all,

And become as bright,

Meet me in surrender,

Meet me with the strength of summer,

United in all and precious tender,

Loving in the breath of the Lover.

O, meet me in the solace of fall,

Meet me at the embrace of memory,

But be present in all,

And in all be glory,

Meet me in the tears of winter,

As our souls are washed away,

In clean waters we hall bathe,

And in the One seize the day.

❋ MOTHER NATURE ❋

May I continue to write you prayers in wings of hope as God does,

And be the whispers of love words upon your lips,

The dawn of awakening in your eyes when the sun becomes your heart,

And the breath of eternity when in my last breath my smile is on your lips,

For angels have known me for writing poems in petals of ecstasy,

And God has guided my hand through the rivers of your soul,

So when dusk arrives,

Memories will be of Him in us that kissed the kiss that will remain.

❋ UNKNOWING ❋

Of north winds I know very little,

Rains of yesterday only that they're gone,

Victories and tragedies all a sight, perhaps not even that in all that is,

But of love my Beloved, but of love

You make me all that I am, and I rejoice.

❋ TRUST ❋

Misplace not your faith sweet brother,

For in the things seen shall always leave your thirst unquenched,

Trust,

Trust the unseen my precious one, and as the breath follows the depths of your heart,

You shall receive the blessings of allowing.

Be aware of love where love must be placed,

In here, and there, the unspoken voice will lead you into the heavens when your silent mind mirrors your kindred heart,

Be of good spirit, for your light shall be the flame that others recognize the beauty of the unknown mystery, as I have in you.

❁ SALVATION ❁

I've wanted to be saved

I've looked in every sun and moonlight

O, how I wanted to be saved

And awakened to the light within

Laughed and cried

Rolled and stood high

Reached to the stars to become my lover

Reached within my heart

Became my own savior

And smiled, and smiled

Let us smile.

❋ Hope ❋

Yet so close, a touch away,

The remembrance of a sight,

The inhalation of a blessing,

Yet, so faraway, when dormant shadows awake,

And the hope falls like cascades of nothingness,

Exhaling the despair of yesterdays,

Returning to the same old blame.

But the hope....

O yes, the hope, yet

Always at hand,

When the butterfly of truth

Takes flight into existence,

And we recognize the salvation from within,

And yet evolves to presence,

Where Divine landscapes are us.

❧ LIFE ❧

What is there for me to know, spaciousness of my heart?

How far does my spirit go?

How close does it stay?

In these spaces of questioning may I kiss the all Knowing?

May I recognize my Beloved self?

The death of each breath is but the awakening of each life,

Each life at every breath taken,

The complete sacrifice of unknowing,

Where revelations of becoming are the forgetfulness of the lie,

Or perhaps a willingness to see it for what it really is.

And movement continues,

Sorrows and lust , all the same flow ,

Healing and cursing, all without judgment,

Dying and living,

Past and future,

Caring nothing for it all is but illusion .

Isn't that right my dear?...

So, again inhale...

And live

Exhale... And die

Return to innocence for your seasons are the beauty of your soul,

One prettier than the other, all equal.

❋ MELODIC ENCOUNTERS ❋

Ordinary rivers

Ordinary lives

Channels of hope streaming through each other's veins

Path of melodic encounters

And the joy of recognizing each other's waters

The beauty of our calm seas

The rewards of our storms

In the eyes of the beholder

Lies the beauty, even if tear-felt

And so the extraordinary rushes through

And in bowing song

We embrace by saying yes

Out of our intimate selves

Just as it was always meant to be.

❧ EMBRACE ❧

Open arms,

Stretched all the way to receive your becoming.

Bowed head I then pray,

That your arriving be the continuation of your path.

For my path only begins when you and you and you

Have recognized my flaws as yours,

Breaking the same bread,

Under the same olive tree of life,

Sour in moments,

Pleasing most of times,

Stepping ever so gently into the embrace of each other again,

Trudging in our mutual walk,

The one where the cup remains full as each one of us keeps on giving

And the drinking is good and sober.

❋ FALLING ❋

I fall yes I fall

Sometimes upward so high that only the sun catches me

Others so deep that only the breath saves me

But I fall sweet brother

I fall

And what miracle that is

That I offer my fall to your eyes

That I offer my fall to your mouth

To your limbs

To your body

That you can know that we fall together

And in the falling of each other

We find each other's healing

Breath in breath

Heal than if my fall calls it so

And the balm of my tears

Heals the heart sores of your hurts.

❄ Oneness ❄

Images of centuries gone by,

Who took the breath that I breathed yesterday?

No one, it remains....

So I shall continue to breathe the same breath of the Father,

All my brethren and I, we all shall continue to be one.

🌸 SOWING 🌸

Seeds in living

Spread by the loving hands of action

In fertile soil may fall

The love intent in the throw of the Creator

Angels gathering in the harvest of knowing

Here, at the feet of Presence

Calling the calling of being

Recognizing oneself in the eyes of my brethren

Seeds of living, seeds of loving

Farmers of love dedicated to the awakening of existence

Now.

❄ Return To Innocence ❄

Come a bit closer,

Dreamer of silence,

I'll give you all that is mine to give,

Breath in hand ,

Color your darkness,

I carry all that in my love you shall give,

And when we dance

The dance of fire,

Let's us recognize our flame,

And as we bless

Blessings of fire,

Let's us return to innocence,

And forgive...

❋ IMMORTALITY ❋

Yes, lay my body in those immortal memories,

As my spirit rests in the promised womb of freedom.

Yes, carve my name in winds of remembrance,

For my soul is now the eternal flame in every prayer.

Yes, melt the voice of my last whisper into a golden frame,

The subtleness of my touch shall be felt in the silence of thunder.

For I have lived,

For I have lived,

For I have Loved.

❁ FORGIVENESS ❁

Rivers dancing

Life awakening

The breath of life came singing into silence

The blood line of forgiveness broke down the wall of apathy

The hand that reaches for the heart, reaches for the waters of Love

Submerged in the essence of being

May we dance, and dance again till forgiveness becomes us.

❀ BLESSINGS ❀

Say your story in greens of pine

Say your longing in turns of silk

May your blessings unfold in curls of incense

Say your dreams in wings of sparrows

Bless us with your gentle moments

Bless us again

Say your blessings in songs of sirens

Say them , say them

Their scent your moment

Your moment, ours

The blessings , our beingness

How great it is to be human

Say your story in our silence

Say it.

🌸 You Are Loved 🌸

The words are few...

The moment remains...

The silence endures...

Falcons brave,

Waters sweet,

Kisses from the Gods,

And the whisper let it be known...You Are Loved.

❀ LOST, NOW FOUND ❀

My brother brought me the gift of forgiveness yesterday

There before me sat a stranger whom I never met before

And in a dance of tears and laughter he told my story

And if there's a count in rain drops, he counts them to me

And if the length between the hearts is measurable, he measures it to me

His life was my life

His breath mine, and present as the Beloved was

I spoke through his lips

My voice was silence

One by one I felt my sins being lifted

The gift was real, I accepted it

My brother's story was my story

And I felt God's kisses all over my face

His love in my heart

At last, life made sense.

Now I know that I'm found.

🌸 Olive Oil 🌸

Novel oil that blesses my soul

What great essence you carry from the time of your first seed,

You have caressed the feet of the Master

And the bread of my brethren

Olive of soul

It's what I call you

Fruit of divine

Legacy of presence

In the years before you have remain available

Like the breath

Always willing to remind us of the Father of Light.

Sweet You Are.

Sweet You Are.

Sweet You Are.

❀ FLAME ❀

Flame, guide me...

Guide me on the blinding path

Guide me unto the inward labyrinth of my own

My own breath

My own forgetfulness

My own knowing of unknown terrain

Flame

Candlelight of eternal oils

Divine lights of small surrenders

Volcanoes of awakening remembrances

Lighthouse of inner waters

Oceans of breath

May my arrival be unbeknownst to me

May your burning remain as I fade.

🏵 Treasure 🏵

I wanted to lose myself

I lost myself

I lost myself completely into Your unknowing, my Beloved.

I lost myself completely in Your unseen-ness, my Beloved.

I found an unknown beauty

I found a beautiful man

I found myself

You always had me.

🌸 THE RUN 🌸

Running fast, faster than breath

As a gazelle from the hungry lion I run

Feet bleeding, same path

Lion closer

Fear near

Keep running, faster now

Nowhere to arrive

Lost in thought

Legs trembling

Changed the path

There is no lion

My feet have healed

I graze in green pastures

I lay in still waters

I changed the path, changed the path

No more running.

❄ THE MERGE ❄

Yes, there's my shadow

Following me faithfully

At every breath, at every turn

Constant, silent

The stronger the light in me

The darker my shadow becomes

It's me

The whole of me

And only love joins us to embrace each other.

❋ CITRUS ❋

Look at this orange peel,

Swirl around the fragrance of awakening,

Eat the joys of morning pulp-filled juicy wedges,

Run in the juices of love,

Be a dancing tree,

A rolling fruit,

An ocean of clouds laughing at the world beneath,

O sweet child.

You, you alone are a fruit unto the Beloved.

Rejoice precious one rejoice.

❄ Storyteller ❄

Closed heart allows no story

The ones that lift one's spirit

Shells of lost dreams and castles of despair

May the waves of sweet oceans break them all

And in mellow shores we lay naked

That the sun of arrival makes us whole again

And the preciousness of our hearts

Be the very suns that heal us

And stories will be told and shared

And tears shall turn to laughter

And dreams to melodies

And the dance of hearts will open us in laced honey kisses

While God simply smiles

All is well.

All is well.

All is well.

🏵 LIGHTHOUSE 🏵

In what shade have you hidden your truth, sweet brother,

That your tears consume you,

That your breath is shallow?

Come, come into the light.

Let me be a lighthouse of hope even if for a moment.

For a lost soul into darkness

Is the fall of us all.

The walk in brightness

Is the joy in each other's life.

May our breath continue to be one

As a smile goes on.

❀ ROSE ❀

Traveler of sorrows,

Come rest your burden in my lap.

May your thought be clear as wind

And your breath light as the one who created you.

Craft not your misery upon your convictions,

But open the rise of your essence to be that of a rose.

Become the fragrance of contentment

As you nap in my embrace,

Safe and secure,

Calm and relaxed,

Here, in the openness of allowing.

❀ ONENESS ❀

Your breath is my breath

Your heart beat mine it is

Through your eyes I see

Through your presence I feel

In my innocence I rejoice

In your love I am

❀ Melanie ❀

Have you left us sweet sister?

Sure you have not,

Your breath remains.

In the wings of memory you travel into the homes of our hearts.

Your departure to love

Is the arrival of the divine.

The remembrance of you,

The visit of Him that abides in our sacredness,

You are here,

You are here,

You are here,

Love You are.

✸ PRAYER ✸

If suffering is the common ground of our loving,

Let me suffer with you.

If silence is the soil that will nourish our healing,

Let me silently sow with you.

If prayer is the water that quenches your thirst,

Let me pour it for you.

If death is what gives me the life that you gave me,

Let me die to myself.

❈ The Breath ❈

What is real?

Is this hand real?

This leg, this face?

Nothing is real but this breath.

This breath that You breathe into me,

When awake to that,

Than I can be real.

Until then, the thought of who I am is but an illusion.

❀ RISING ❀

Vibrant Rising

Vibrant Rose

Expand within me Your fragrance

That my being be but Your perfume

Explode within my Heart

That the rays of fire be the open petals of Your compassion

And my smile Your rapture

Vibrant Rising indeed

When I rejoice in the forgetfulness of my name

And call Yours as mine

And all that is Yours is mine

My death Yours

Your Life mine

And so it is.

❁ LAMP ❁

You shall not extinguish this fire with the waters of your judg-
ment.

Sweet brother, from what rivers are you soaking

That my lamp blinds you into rage?

I am but a pilgrim,

Sure never to question your path.

So return to innocence, if you may,

And may we play together

So that both our lights warm the world.

Please join me in quenching our thirst from the Unknown Well

And swim in this ocean of Fire.

❧ THE GIFT ❧

Will you let me buy your suffering?

I'll buy it with the gold of mine.

Will you sell me your joys?

I buy them with the silver of mine.

Will you share your God?

I share it with the silence of mine,

And may we continue remaining as one.

❀ DIVINITY ❀

If water, mist shall become of me

If stone, dust

Wood, ashes

And so I am human,

And so I weep and hail,

Laugh, smile,

Till the day comes

Where mist and dust

And ashes

Become You, You are the tears of such humanness,

And in all that I am, divinity is, with all that surrounds me.

❄ MAGNIFICAT ❄

They fall

They fall

Unheard whispers

Spoken in Magnificat

I held Your bleeding body

I clean Your wounds

I tend to You

These tears fall

They fall in recognition

Forgive me Father

For I am the assailant.

❀ Name ❀

Nursing my breath in subtle wakefulness,

Nourishing my longing for You in deeper sighs,

I have heard many of Your names.

To all of them I respond, silent , just silent.

If ice were to be my essence,

My coolness would be You.

If fire were the heat that consumed me,

I would carve Your name in the skies

With the smoke of my abandonment.

And so, You…

You are so faraway, yet so close,

So distant, yet piercing my heart with ongoing hunger,

So present that I fool myself into calling You my name,

So abandoned to Your beauty, to Your profound Love,

I shall continue to call You.

And again, I breathe.

I awaken.

I sigh.

❋ NIGHTINGALE ❋

Nightingale, brother of life,

You carry the stardust of my Beloved in your wings,

You visit my spirit and awake I am to your song,

The veils of illusion are distant memories,

You bring the force of immortality,

I am on my knees,

The prayer is everlasting,

I, too, fly now upon your roar.

❀ ANGER ❀

Sweet anger,

Here you are, letting me know that I, too, am human.

Sweet anger,

I will embrace you with love and compassion,

For if not, you'll kill me with silent scorn.

❋ ASCENDING ❋

Lullabies and songs of contemplation

Blossom roses in gardens of joy

The Beloved smiles

The crowd becomes still

The breath led the procession of intent

And the children planted kisses on elderly

The lion sat in repose next to the lamb

We all drank from the abundance of the same well

One leper healed all others with compassion

And he himself ascended

We cried in joyful bliss

And broke bread together

Welcome home.

Welcome home.

Welcome home.

🌸 BEAUTY 🌸

The voice of the seed calling

The coming into the center of wisdom

I have been placed in the womb

Warm, and recalling the beauty of being

Just being

Flowering in essence

An essence in Christ

Into the breath of all that He is

I Am.

❋ BREATH OF LIFE ❋

An openness

A moment

Let the stillness of this breath be my truth

Even if perhaps convinced by a momentary lapse of reason

Even the illusion shall be transformed

Where the spirit abides the light swells

All that is comes forth in ultimate reality

Regardless of my little plans

The Divine will prevail

I trust that

I know that

I continue within the breath of life

All is well.

All is well.

All is well.

❀ Suffering ❀

I hurt

The silence has overtaken me

I cannot recall my name

My face has vanished

My breath is still

The pain is the lie

My mind is quiet

I hurt

"Stop"

I hear it said

Who's saying it?

I'm still

I exhale

I'm here

I persist

I become we

We Are.

❈ Prayer ❈

Creator,

May I become the waters that quench my brother's thirst when the droughts of self have dried his spirit,

Father of Light,

May I become the tree that shades my brother's body when the heat of desperation consumes his hopes.

Beloved,

May I become the rock on which my tired brother rests when the fights of illusion have exhausted him.

Divine Mother,

May I become the rose whose fragrance becomes my brother's solace when the stench of denial has overtaken him.

Almighty,

May I become the lamp whose light may guide my brother to You when all darkness has overcome him.

And Lord,

I pray to You sweet Presence of Life,

That when blinded you give me Your sight,

When deaf you give Your hearing,

When asleep You wake me up,

That I, too, die to my lies,

And surrender to the Love that You offer me in my brother,

And we shall walk hand in hand in Your everlasting freedom.

Amen.

❀ SURRENDER ❀

Solemn is the unvoiced truth.

Sorrow is the voice of the unheard.

Remember a breath in vastness

And consider descending into your own reality.

The promise is your own awakening.

Savant in the slow living of sorrow we had become,

But within is the bursting fire of truth leading us to gentleness,

Leading to Beauty,

The greatest surrender into the Beloved.

May in Love we take another breath

And honor the blessed gift of life.

Yea though we walk through the shadows of the valley of death,

We bring forth the light,

A light trusted to us from the healing joys of the Creator.

❀ Meek ❀

Weed growing seeds of illusion

An enemy called happiness

Shouts from higher mountains

"Hey come and get me; I am all you must live for."

While the unspoken gentleness of contentment rests in still water banks,

Evokes the loving presence of the breath,

Saying,

"I am already here, all love, all yours,

Blessed are the meek..."

❋ BALLAD ❋

The Father spoke:

"Would you let me Love you my little one,

Will you let me embrace you with the softness of quietness,

Fulfill you with the mastery of esteem,

Bless you with omnipotence of healing,

Cradle you in peaceful emotions and reward you with your true self?

Come, come to me in the silence of your humbleness,

Come, come to me in your child like playfulness,

Come, come to me with a empty basket of expectations,

And let your gentle being be.

For in Me you are

And Love you become

And Love you shall remain."

🏵 DREAM 🏵

Knights of hope surround this humble table,

In silence the prayer is evoked,

Green spreads through valleys,

The sky color matches the quiet ocean within,

In a moment smiles abound,

The festivity of love has begun.

The knights dropped their swords,

Beasts and man played in harmony,

Brethren shared bread abundantly.

Joy became the main unspoken presence...

Once upon a time I told a dream to a child, and we both believed it,

And it was good,

It was very good....

❀ SELF ❀

I've hidden my soul

Behind the thousand masks of self.

I have betrayed my Beloved.

My thoughts have become the ruler of dawn.

A tyrant master, the mind, has turned against the preciousness of being.

I walk in darkness,

Darkness walks in me,

And until the lesson is learned,

I am but a slave of my suffering self.

I must say yes.

❀ GRACE ❀

I now crawl from under the rock of darkness,

I free myself from the burden of blindness,

For a moment I believed I was the one doing it.

And for a moment I almost crawled back from where I had been free,

But Your shining light, O Almighty,

Keeps on burning the lies within,

And so it is that the path becomes clear,

From a crawling fool, now a walking fool,

A fool never the less.

Great to know that Your light remains.

❋ FORGIVENESS ❋

Who are you who betrays me?

The ruthless liar of presence?

How did you come into my house and claim my peace?

When and where have we met?

I see...

You tell me that the moment I claim a life lived on self will,

I claimed You as myself,

I now bow to my humanness,

For forgiveness must begin within.

Shalom, shalom, shalom.

❋ Loneliness ❋

Lonesome is the man that trudges without You.

The rivers dry,

The skies darken, as the sun recoils in sadness,

And the moon hides in shame.

All is but an abyss of chaos,

And it is in there that desperation becomes bliss,

And the man regains sight

For the waters of hope rush in.

The sun of life bursts open the darkness of denial,

The sister moon brings the nurturing comfort of presence,

And loneliness is transformed in solitude,

And You, my Beloved, become the man, as he becomes You.

❀ THE RIVERS INSIDE ❀

Enter, enter sweet brother

The waters of love are cooling in here

Bless yourself in the harmony of much presence

Allow these rivers to take you inside

Enter, enter sweet brother

No other love can sway you as this one does

These waters quench and cleanse

No drinking necessary

No swimming either

So cry... cry sweet brother

Let those sorrows run through and through

Gentle waters coming forth

Healing is their birth

Cry so cry

That the freshness of this letting go

May gift you with the joys of stillness

And in her embrace

A gentle path shall emerge

Recognition of the Divine within.

❈ Meditation ❈

Formless breath of awakening,

Take this fool out of his slumber.

I am the ridicule of wanting,

And the callings of the wild,

Let my knees be bloody in prayer,

For I am done with the walks of limelight.

I'll keep silent to false gods,

I'll keep silent to false gods,

I must

Or my death will be one of living suffering,

To which I refuse to die.

I'll die to You formless breath,

Just this one more time until I'll inhale again and kiss my Beloved.

❋ PEACE ❋

A meeting with peace

Face to face

Heart to heart

The knowing of the unknown

Remaining present

Cascades of surreal emotions

The warriors of Maia

Traveling in and out of this mansion

They seek recognition

All is well

They leave

Touching silence with blissful breath

Mindless awake

Warmth, certainty

Inhaling hope in an open white canvas

A meeting with peace

Indeed,

Coming home is just that.

Welcome Home.

Welcome Home.

Welcome Home.

❈ SURRENDER ❈

This heart of dawn

An open lotus to the birth of pure love

My bow is one with the hurt of my brethren

My surrender is one with the tears of lost mothers

My silence is one with the loudness of mad men weeping

I understand,

Pure Love is born of the awareness

Nakedness in spirit

A mirror of us, all of us

And when night falls,

We can whisper the songs of forgiveness

A moment in the solace of truth,

Divine it is in all that is.

❋ ROYAL GOLDEN ❋

How many miles are there?

Sitting at the seat of my soul

I become the observer of the vastness within

How far does this love stretch?

How many boundaries will break?

The royal golden aiming is the unseen.

Here, I am one with the great teacher,

The silence

The lover

Miles and miles

A distance of untouched terrain

A wild one that is

Attackers at every breath

But so much love in it

One more breath,

One more breath,

After all, I am home indeed.

❄ BECOMING ❄

Come, come

Enter this place of immortality

Jump in these waters of bliss

Fall into this knowing of unknown

This sacred beingness that awakes us to each other,

The walking path of unity

Where the spirit binds us,

And we finally surrender to our oneness,

Come, come,

Be the rose in me

Come, come,

Be the mother of my words

Come, come,

Be the rivers of my dreams

And when all is said and done,

Let's be God together.

❋ THE QUESTION ❋

Sweet brother your wisdom abided in my heart tonight,

The words of the Beloved were your words,

"When suffering remains, are you willing to go on, knowing that I Am with you?"

My mind stayed still,

Your gentle smile became one with the joys of my heart,

Sacredness met in union in a simple question,

To you sweet brother I bow,

How grateful I am for you.

❋ Allowing ❋

Resist no evil, said the good Master,

Indeed sweet brother,

That which we resist, persists

Allow the awareness of unkind thoughts to travel as tides,

Clouds that navigate in the inconsistency of the mind,

Just that

Let them be

And be here, now

Be here with the divine presence of breath

Contentment at hand.

❀ LETTING GO ❀

What precious death, this one to the unknowing,

A death on each breath,

A communion with a life of mystery,

I unlearn, and know,

I un-see, and envision,

I un-grasp, and am overtaken by the grace that breathes me.

What sweeter death, this one

This one where I am one with an unattended, unassumed rose,

Anonymous, in her solace,

Manifesting beauty just because it is what it is meant to be,

Dying, undiscovered, content,

I'm the simplicity of nothingness

Bowing in presence.

❀ Lotus ❀

Flowers of distance

Lotus of within

The fragrance of dawn rests upon my sacredness,

And my disbelief melts as mist.

The water fountain of the unseen keeps on quenching my thirst.

I drink, I drink again,

I am not satisfied, neither do I want to be.

I let the roots of this beingness grow deeper,

The leafs of hope spring higher,

How immortal is the vastness of all,

I bow.

The mystery of You is but the reality me.

❀ REBORN ❀

The moment that I am reborn

I become the willow that always was

The dance of leaves entertaining the Beloved

The humming of the storm into the branches

Solid in feeling

Thought navigating thru waters of mindless existences

Going, coming back, waves crashing into shore, nothing more

It is what waves do in the end, after all

The nourishment of rains as the new life rushes in

How grateful is this Oak tree

Did I say Oak tree?

What happen to the willow?

Never mind the symbol I insist in creating

Reborn I am to the adamantine essence of existence

Truly awake.

❀ HERE ❀

I awake into the heart of this tree

I am here

I awake into the silence of this lake

I am here

I awake into the presence of this buffalo

I am here

I awake into the gentleness of this hummingbird

I am here

I awake to the caressing of this wind

I am here

I awake to that man that is reflecting my eyes

I am here.

I am here.

❋ HANDS ❋

Look at this these hands

Look at them, held together

Held in a hope vision called prayer

Called surrender

Called desperation

O sweet arrival at the sweet gates of darkness when finally light becomes

Look at this these hands

Palm against palm

And the silence of knowing

That now, yes now all will be well for the descending has stopped

The only way is up

And so this prayer goes

As in death becomes life

And life finishes her cycle with so much love.

❀ GUARDIAN ❀

Yes Father

I am guarding Your light

Not under the closed doors of temples

But in open arms of sky windows

An eternal flame of caring love

Of sweet compassion

Of never-ending forgiveness

That myself be lost in You.

All of that is me becoming nothing more than You,

Let it shine.

Let it shine.

❀ FOLLOW ME ❀

The call is subtle

Yet so real.

Follow me, I hear

Follow me,

Let your garments down,

Place your hands high,

Lift your heart,

Follow me.

I shall.

❀ THE CALLING ❀

The calling has come from the winds of the west,

The calling has come from the winds of the east,

The calling has come from the heights of the mountains,

The calling has come from the depth of the oceans.

My heart explodes in ecstasy,

The truth has arrived from beyond all,

My heart surrendered in subtle recognition,

For He has done the calling all along.

May I never forget to see the calling in my brother's eyes,

To recognize the calling in my brother's heart.

Amen.

❋ WITHIN ❋

O, but it's out there

It's ugly and muggy

It's dirty

It's dirty

Out there it is

But I am here

It is here I must look

O, but it is dark

It is scary

Dare to look

Dare to stay

It shall become light

As within, without

And it will be preciously beautiful

It must begin with me

I must say yes.

🌸 Strawberries And Cream 🌸

Strawberries and cream

How foolish of me

Must silence become the view of these wounds?

I must say yes,

So the evolving of this soul travels in paths of suffering,

Indeed,

But I wanted strawberries and cream,

They are here,

Yes they are,

Savoring them in the spaces in between,

The one where the inhale meets my exhale,

And You, gentleness of creation, simply smile,

And I become what I always was,

You.

❁ Child ❁

O my Beloved,

I've been kissed by the joys of jealousy,

I weep,

In the stillness of this humanness of mine I observe

What different fire forges this gentle spirit,

I smile,

What joys, the ones of being,

I observe,

Let my fears be the coals of emerging,

Let Your love be the balm of my existence,

I come to You as a child,

Thank You for cradling me in Your lap.

❃ Your Name ❃

They wanted your name

They demanded it

They wanted to own it and to hold it in their hands as if it were
a rock

I begged them to sit

They became loud

They wanted Your name

So I sat, and remained silent.

And one by one they sat and remained silent.

Soon they found Your name

Yes there is the unspoken truth

I am with You and I know it

I say Your name and I know it

I share my smile and I know it

I give Your Love

In Your love, Your name

And everyone knows it.

❀ KINDNESS ❀

Do not take my kindness for weakness sweet brother

I am but a man after all

And my blood is as red as yours

My skin as thin as yours

My soul as precious as yours

So be awake to reason sweet brother

Be aware of being willing to take all that comes with it

For even Christ had a temper

Help me follow His steps, closely

Then again, look into your own soul

And find the joys of the Master

My forgiveness and love is yours to share

Truly in abundance.

❊ Vessel ❊

You who breathes me

Allows me to look at my walls of silence

I study them

I hear them

You who breathes me

Allows me to trust my senses

To honor my memories

To value this vessel

Your vessel

Named my body

I come to know and celebrate the truth,

The truth in all of us

In all that is

So You breathe me

A life larger than vastness

A breath deeper than depth

You, You who breathes me

Have come to call me again

And in my listening

I bow.

I bow.

I bow.

❀ Punisher ❀

Guard me from the assailant, O Master of light

Protect me from the abuser, O Lord of Divinity

Spare me from the judge and the punisher,

And from the evil doer,

O my Beloved,

How I crawl into a ball of nothingness

And the attackers go in merciless,

On my knees I beg You, sweet Creator,

Save me from myself, the greatest enemy of all,

May my death become a light,

A lighthouse to all,

May the forgiveness of your existence transpire in my surrender,

May I be the saving raft,

The rope that is offered,

As the offenders melt into your golden truth of what I am,

And I remain standing as the oak tree of nakedness.

❀ RIGHTOUSNESS ❀

What language was that my sweet brother?

You say you speak in the words of God,

I am hurt to hear that that god would say such things about women,

About a man that embraces love differently than you claim doing,

About a nation that prays in a different love language than the one you claim your nation does,

And blessed are thee, you say,

For you claim doing the work of the same God,

I am hurt to see your god hurting his creation.

Forgive my ignorance again,

Please do,

Maybe your god should meet my

God,

And He is not mine either you see,

He is the God that shines His light on all of us the same,

That rains his waters on all of us the same,

That cradles our suffering in his lap,

The same.

I bless you.

❀ Everywhere ❀

And yes I now remember.

Who turns the sunflower to her Beloved sun,

Who guides the salmon to swim up the stream,

Who calls the bee to pollinate thy flower,

And who holds the hummingbird in the strength of his wings.

Let us stop now and breathe.

O sweet brother, the making of a small god has placed a canyon between us,

I'll keep on sharing the beauty of my Master with you,

For how could I ever hide him?

I must smile,

He is everywhere,

Everywhere He is,

And yes, yes, in you too.

❀ MOON ❀

I know now,

The reflection of sister moon is the reflection of You,

The cry of the birthing mother is Your cry,

The hailing of the fathers mourning death is Your hailing,

The laughter of the joyful sunrise is Your laughter,

When understanding emerges, it is You behind the smile,

When innocence is robbed, it is You behind the forgiveness,

When hearts are broken, it is You behind the mending,

When all is nonsense, it is You behind the miracle,

And there's always the miracle,

The one of the birth,

The one of the pardon,

The one of the loving,

The one of the patience,

And the one of the caring, and healing, and listening, and relating, aging, laughing, painting,

Singing, being being being.

O but Christ, as the reflection of sister moon....

It is a miracle indeed when I recognize your reflection behind these eyes of mine,

This smile of mine,

This hurt of mine,

This bowing of mine,

This breath of mine,

As You Are

In all that is,

So it is and shall be that

I Am.

❋ The Calling ❋

You have called me from the most sordid places,

I listened.

You have called me from the most dark places,

I have heard you.

You have called me from the most desperate places,

I called out to you.

You have called me from the most wounded places,

I came to find you,

And I found you, indeed I found you.

And you were clothed in rich garments and dressed in rags,

And the color of your skin was as transparent as the beauty of your eyes,

And your age was ageless,

And your sex non-existent,

Simply because when you called,

You spoke my language,

The language of the heart,

Where bliss meets suffering

And death becomes life,

And so it is Father of Light

That You keep on calling me to these places,

And out of sheer adoration for You I am but the beggar,

Begging You,

Call me, call me, I am here,

Call me, call me, I shall continue answering the call,

I shall continue saying yes.

❋ PRAYER ❋

Dear Lord, do not allow the waters of my reasoning to stand between the light of your glory and my brothers existence,

Dear Lord, do not allow the hurricanes of my will to stand in between the omnipotence of your miracles and my brothers healing,

Dear Lord, do not allow the storms of my judgment to stand between the touch of your enlightenment and my brothers surrender,

Dear Lord, do not allow the fury of my arrogance to stand between the lovingness of your presence and my brothers' birth into a new life,

And save me, O Father,

From the fears of the unknown,

That I may be completely in your presence,

From the lashes of wrong thinking,

That I may recognize your presence,

From the wounding of my actions,

That I carry your presence,

From the lying of my own entitlement,

That I may be Your Presence,

Amen.

❀ Pilgrim ❀

Wisdom is to be found in the unknown.

That is right.

Wisdom is to be found in the unbreakable darkness,

In the gifts of desperation,

In the silence of unreason,

And, alas,

The gift of life emerges,

The unbreakable becomes light,

The unknown remains silent in the soul's alchemy now named "humility,"

Robbing one's experience of such is the greatest sin,

No one can leave the foot prints for the pilgrim.

For the gift is in the trudging,

And then, let it be light,

And it is good.

❀ VAGABOND ❀

Yes I know, I am ignorant to divine things,

I know very little of the words in the good books,

I am but a vagabond in the darkness of spirit,

Seeking the light,

Seeking the light.

Will my willingness open the gates of love to bless me?

And as I seek, is my seeking enough in the winds of wisdom?

Does my Beloved embrace my nakedness and simplicity into His
bosom and cradle my head in caring adoration?

He already has,

And the path as only begun,

Yes, I don't know much,

All I know is that Love has touched me.

❁ COURAGE ❁

Courage, courage, I hear the voice within

Don't do it, you will fail, I hear the voices of yesterday's

The coolness of the body makes the soul believe the lies.

Courage, courage,

One more step in the right path,

If the breath is of God,

I am breathing Him in and out.

Courage, courage,

The dream is at hand,

The sweet taste of being it,

Being the dream that is,

The breath of life is already the dream fulfilled.

Courage, courage,

Don't do it, stop now, who do you think you are???

I am the one that carries the life force of God's promises,

I breathe therefore I am,

I feel therefore I am.

Courage, courage,

Hand in hand with all that is,

Dreams do come true.

❋ NAME ❋

I wrote His name in fig trees

Dear me

I wrote His name everywhere

In fig trees, in temple doors

I wrote His name in church bells

And in symphonies, and in school tables

They called me mad

I called myself that to.

And the day I wrote His name in my heart

I fell silent,

No more writing,

The Beloved is home.

🏵 Peach 🏵

I peeled my Lord a peach,

I sat, I watched,

The juices ran down,

My mouth watered,

I took a bite, It was good,

I finished,

It was wonderful,

I guess the peach was meant to be for me.

Thank you, Father.

❋ GRATITUDE ❋

The tree is rich

The fruit is succulent

The rains abide and the sun brings growth,

The harvest is abundant.

How magnificent is your tree sweet brother?

Are you awake to the joys of your fruits?

Is your head bent down seeking the spoiled ones?

We all have them you know.

Be of good joy and gratitude for the Great Farmer keeps on giving,

Allow the land of your generosity,

Be the presence of your gratefulness,

And smile onto the abundance of the bounty of your branches.

Sweet fruits, indeed, sweet brother,

Sweet fruits indeed...

❈ Fool ❈

The wonders of deception

Hiding in the shadows shall not make you invisible, sweet brother,

Come, come step into the light,

You may squint, you may curse,

And our God rejoices in all of it.

We will never be rendered white as snow,

But surely we can dance in the rain,

Jump up and down in the puddles,

Be like children, just the way He wants us.

I know sweet brother; I know the comfort of the lie,

The lie that whispers us into the hiding,

But I also know the glory of the sunshine in our smiling faces when the shadow is embraced.

Fear not looking like a fool

For the Beloved, I'd rather be a fool than a self righteous stick.

❊ MORTAR OF LOVE ❊

Yes my reincarnation will be that of a song,

The one that speaks of holy longing,

The psalm that leaves the ongoing tear rolling till taste becomes communion,

The prayer that will not cease and turn to a thunder tide of indigo waters of only one ocean,

The cry into the wilderness of heart, the unspoken poem of delirium over one's Beloved.

Yes, my reincarnation will be opium incense in the temples of dawn, the perfume of nostalgia in the scarf of the hidden shadow within,

The mortar of love,

The sands of sights

The last breath into the new life.

❈ Man In The Mirror ❈

There, there, do you see it sweet brother?

There, those are the eyes of Christ in disguise,

Listen to the words of sorrow behind that bravado,

See the little child in need of affection behind that mask of anger,

Observe the lost soul behind all that knowing,

Now come, bow with me if you would like,

May a prayer within our heart free us to experience the Beloved,

May the gentleness of compassion be the birth from the Beloved Mother,

Towards the man in the mirror.

🌼 BREAD 🌼

Yes, I became the flour under your hands,

Yes, I became the water under your hands,

Yes, I became the dash of salt and sugar under your hands,

And you fermented me,

And you kneaded me,

And you twisted and turned me around,

And you watch me there, you watch me be

In the fire where you placed me,

In the fire where you purified me,

In you I became the bread of life

Which I feed my brethren.

O how merciful you are.

❀ Stillness ❀

Solace, solace, solace,

In a pillow of solitude you have laid me,

Comforted, in lavender scented linen you covered me,

My nakedness, Your silence,

My sleep, Your dream,

I repose in the rainy waters of autumn falls,

And her red leafs falling into my illusions

With the sparse greens of hope.

Your whisper arrives at dusk

When I awaken into the lies of restlessness

"Be Still..."

I dance into the gaze of my shadow,

I sing into the candlelight of song,

The one that the prophet never wrote,

"A guiding light ...You are..."

My Beloved came to celebrate my solace with me...

"Welcome, welcome."

Let these words be the praise my heart offers

For my lips are closed to such ecstasy.

❀ PHOENIX RISING ❀

Under the phoenix ashes

My song became that of a nightingale

Sweet in the sorrow

Bitter in the reawakening

Founded in temple ruins

Mourned in mosques of prayer.

My song evokes the Beloved within

Where life simply is,

Is a day under the sun,

Is an evening of dance,

And when ashes settle,

Is a melody of passion.

Christ swirls with me,

Hand in hand while the reed keeps on ailing,

And we both fall onto the ground,

Laughing silly,

Hugging as,

Healing with each clean breath of tender hope.

The bird has risen,

So has my soul,

And from the gifts of desperation,

So as the son,

I followed the path.

Sweet song still remains upon my lips.

🏵 GIFT OF DESPERATION 🏵

I have crowned myself with illusions,

Dressed in royal dresses of thin air,

Drunken from the oasis of emptiness,

And in its waters swam into never-lands of despair.

There, I ate coals for meals,

And yelled silently until the bitter sweet tears took courage on emerging.

There, in lands of nowhere,

I wrote the words onto the unspoken till my voice hurt.

And there in that covered up nakedness, You just could not stop loving me,

And You Said:

"ENOUGH... Enough child, enough , you are a motherless child no longer, you are a fatherless child no longer, Be Still Now... I Am here."

O my gentle fingers tremble,

I plunge into the midst of all of You,

I regain my breathe,

Yes, Father of Light,

Yes, Mother of Healing,

Your Love has taken away my pain which I thought was my sin.

Blessed Are Thee,

Rose petals carry but a fraction of your essence,

They're yours, nevertheless ...

As I am.

❁ THE RESIDENT ❁

Northwinds, Northlands,

Calling from within,

My step is fragile

But I am trudging,

The morning bell cries for my awakening,

I am listening,

The breath is still,

And the morning unfolding.

The Beloved has laid before me the table of life,

I am to feast in her bosom,

Winds soar,

My heart follows,

Heavy or not , it follows

Into those northlands of unknowing,

It follows

Into those northwinds of uncertainty,

It follows,

And when night falls,

The bow is subtle,

But it is there.

Home again,

Home again,

Distant land

Never left,

Christ has made His residence within the canyons of my heart.

Breathe...breathe...

❈ HEALING WATERS ❈

Oh waters of despair,

You came to wash my illusions away,

You came to turn happiness into contentment,

You came to turn arriving into seeking,

Self into un-self,

Thoughts to feelings,

And I am ready to fight Your currents of wisdom.

I will be fighting with You and I know I shall continue

But less, precious waters,

Much less,

For deep within I know of Your love,

I know of Your care,

Of your Divine cleansing,

Waters of heaven turned to fire.

I drink from your fountain,

The Flames of surrender overtake me,

I lose strength and it is good,

I am healing…

❀ Seeds Of Hope ❀

Ruins, they call them, ruins,

Lost seeds of hope...

Lost seeds of hope?

Yes, ruins, maybe.

And, if so, let them be,

Let the rains of love fall

From any distant cloud that makes her journey into salvation,

Share her loving drops of tenderness,

Let these seeds soak in the warm embrace of care,

The breath of life shall remain.

See these "lost seeds of hope" gently sprout...

And look, look, look how the rays of belief shine upon them,

See the tenderness of father-mother sun,

How it cradles them into self-esteem, into trust...

Observe, the shy little sprouts becoming branches of wisdom,

Roots of soundness,

Trees of Life,

Reflections of Divinity...

Because a loving soul, a precious seed,

Fell in love with the ruins,

Recognized her brokenness, and spoke:

"Lost seed of hope no more, the Light of Eternity is present and I shall Love You till your joys of divine success and beyond, because someone has loved me, and my tree stands stronger. "

✸ ABIDE ✸

Yes, I'm the salt

Yes, I'm the water

The soil in His hands, I am

The Breath in His lungs, I am

Wind as it is, I become

Farming lands, I flourish

Fertile as mother's womb, I nourish

Delicate soft bread, the warm comfort of His taste

Soulful meal, I must

And in the forests I elate in green

And in the skies I burst in thunders

In the mountains the snow becomes my words

His words

These words

Broken open into the Beloved

Salt and honey

Awaken into the silent murmur of divine bliss

I abide.

❀ MAGIC ❀

What magic do I speak off?

I speak of the magic of no magic

I use this word so that my humanness

And your humanness can relate

But it is no magic sweet brother

It's a fall into the never endingness

It's the cry to the endless sorrow

It's the bleeding of the unscarred wound

It's the inhaling under water

The gasping for death

The encounter of the sweetness of Christ

That we fall into the knowing

That we cry into the joy

That we bleed into healing

That we breathe into holiness

That we surrender to the preciousness of life

And the magic becomes miracle

And the magic becomes divine

And divinity is you

And divinity is me

And then we just sit there and let Wednesdays be

And warm noons come

And the breaking of the bread is good

It is good indeed sweet brother

It is good because it is human

So please, I beg you sweet brother

Celebrate your humanness with me.

With us.

With Him.

❀ WEAVING ❀

The joys of owning nothingness

Part with the world and in the allowing of the moment

I celebrate being perfectly imperfect,

As You made me,

In my brokenness You planted an orchid,

In my flaws You created rivers of hope,

In my sorrows You set forth a shining light,

Healing Light,

In this grain of sand, I recognized You, me.

Miraculous form of beingness,

Almighty breath of Love,

Waterfall of pleasantness,

Touch of Light,

Bright,

So bright,

The soul dances in between the breaths

And your weaving creates a tapestry of wonder,

Words are to lose their meaning,

The gaze reckons the truth,

Unspoken.

Horses gallop in celestial fields,

Horses bringing forth the solid knowing of awe,

This essence of Yours,

This perfume, this intoxicating perfume of Yours , O Father,

I am on my knees ... Just smiling.

I know that You Are,

You Are,

You Are,

And from that that You are I Am.

❀ WEDNESDAY REMEMBERANCE ❀

Awake into the fullness of emptiness,

Guarding every breath as if it will be the last,

Retaining the silence within as to protect it from the very thinking that might destroy me,

Memory paths, mercy on the walk

That left these feet bleeding.

Can such Calvary be real?

My garments fear my skin,

The light calls as an invitation to opening,

How can one be happy in happiness when despair as been the very sustenance of being?

Awaken to another breath...

Fear not, fear not,

The slaying of ages past is the path to becoming immortal.

I must feel, please let me feel,

Barely exhaling, thinking might just leave me,

Self Love might just become the balm for this man,

Let it all be an unspoken prayer,

For my arms can no longer extend,

My hands touch,

My lips sing to You.

This time Father, You must come and meet me at the fall,

I am tired, too tired,

I am feeling it,

I have begun to feel,

May I rest my head on your lap,

As I did, that hot summer day under the olive tree?

Would you please...

🏵 ROLLING STONES 🏵

Rolling stones, rolling stones,

Nothing more than dust in the wind,

The burden is lifted in the breath of life,

You my Lord become my wings,

I become the foam of your ocean,

These rolling stones that intended to crush me

Have become silly matter, for my heart rejoices.

You are here,

I rest on your sands,

Resting foam

In Your ocean of life.

❀ MEADOWS ❀

Come to know the freedom of the meadows sweet brother

Let yourself be the palm tree

Bent until your bones cry out mercy

May your leafs be prayer flags onto the horizon

And the brothers you call beasts seek shade under your branches.

Have you ever wondered what we shall become once the force of life finds another vessel?

Indeed, sweet brother, indeed,

Ashes to ashes,

But not too soon,

In your love become the beauty of what is,

Life is the golden word,

The word

On which we lay our heads on this grass

And our sighs say...

Amen...amen...amen...

❉ SILENCE REMAINS ❉

How deep is the sound of the unknowing,

The page is turned,

The story changes only to be reflected onto herself,

The realization that all has been just as it was meant to be,

And so it is the silence remains.

The louder one, as quiet as momentarily breath,

Agreeing with destiny,

Saying yes to the unfolding of the soul,

With all her shapes and roughness and the subtle magic of tenderness,

That one that seems to arrive when all seems lost and bound to despair,

How loud are the depths of unknowing,

For when the Beloved cries out our name,

All walls of lies crumble in the presence of such Love.

Unspoken, most silent, most sweet,

So sweet that death itself is but an awakening.

❀ Scholar ❀

Of the divine world, very little I know.

Of wants, I am a scholar,

An insatiable beast with fangs into the flesh of the world,

The victim of self,

The blinded golden man,

But than you allow all to settle ever so gently into the heart of this warrior of silent storms.

You know his voice is as loud as a feather dropping in ocean waters,

No sound, no sound he makes,

No sound I make,

For my own words I swallow with the aid of my tears.

I've seen the Father and He let's me be, He let's me be,

And so I am all that I believe I must be,

And what you believe I must be,

Until I can't be anymore,

And the fall is that not of a feather but of a child,

And so I run to catch him,

And I hold him,

Comfort him,

And in the presence if the Beloved I ask forgiveness

For having forgotten him,

And the Father observes,

And it is good.

I am beginning to feel.

❊ AFFAIR ❊

In your tree of life

I've become your fruit of yearning.

The presence that is yours, the pulp within my skin,

The flow of the eternal Love that is You is but the drop of this juice you've named compassion,

And the leafs of forgiveness shall continue to fall when time calls the ripening of the imposed iron curtains of righteousness.

Blessed are the poor in spirit indeed,

For my body is open to your seed

That I may continue a pregnant affair with You.

Seasons will be seasons,

And I know you'll continue watering my fragile roots,

I shall bend to your winds,

I shall hold to your daughter's soil,

I shall sing with brother wind

That song of yearning remembrance

❀ SACRED HEART ❀

In this moment in all that is true

I'll muster the courage

In my arms I'll carry you

Man or woman

Elderly or child

In the comfort of my embrace

I'll bring you home

Out of the wild

I'll sooth your suffering

That loneliness and desperation

Let my words be the loving

That will heal that separation

That separation that places us apart

In this time of the year

I'll give you my sacred heart

And shed light in your fear

Know my loving child of the creator

That you are never alone

My love for you goes out in a prayer

And meets you in the healing silence that I call Home.

❄ THE ANSWER ❄

Got the answer from above

Got the answer from inside

That the answer is love

That the answer is life

And the glory that surpasses

All understanding

It's the caring that we share

It's the smile we are sharing

Comfort and blessings

In the suffering we gain

Peace and guidance

In the embrace we came

To become, to realize

That the birth and the death

Free us in the love of the Christ.

❁ TITHING ❁

Blessed you are, for your offer to the Beloved is most loving,

Yes my dear one, you offer a day out of your week to the divine,

I heard you well...you said your week... you said, you do the giving...

Alas, God must be so overjoyed.

Me? No sweet brother, I fail miserably in my discipline,

But to His week, I give Him every day,

To His day, I give him every moment,

To His moment, I give Him every breath,

Then I fall again,

Invariably in His loving arms.

For I am but a sinner,

Seeking His loving presence in every breath,

Falling, giving to Him all that I am

Invariably in His loving arms,

Yes, invariably in His loving arms,

Blessings, blessings, blessings to you

O faithful brother, blessings.

❄ Lover Of Life ❄

Lover of life,

Bless thee,

What alms you bring into my home sweet brother,

Just now in the world, you were malicious, unkind...evil??

So I hurt deeply....

And here you are, in my home, sitting in the seat of my sacred heart,

With your sacred heart open, like a pomegranate,

Seeds rolling down, tears following, yours and mine...

Lover of life,

I so have judged you, and kept the veil down...

You bring me the freedom of indigo skies,

In the grace of compassion you shower me,

As if stars were moments of intimate truth, and they are...

My blindness made the Beloved weep,

You sweet brother have healed a foolish blind man, just with your own suffering...

I thank you for the sharing,

For being the mirror...

Your alms shall remain...

I bow to you sweet brother,

I bow to you.

❀ Calvary ❀

The marks of despair still gaze at the next breath...

Are you having a love affair with survival my dear one?

I hear the whisper ...

Does one climb a mountain for the mountain or for the climbing?

Does one love for the Beloved or for the self?

And if love comes in a deeper canyon, will I let myself fall?

Crash into the unknowing , be satisfied with the bleeding and climb again?

I've seen your face, oh Christ,

My survival is no longer a romance but a breath into You,

Calvary ? Yes, I celebrated my own,

And mid-day the hours stopped,

Silence reigned,

You asked me what I wanted,

And I cried,

You, You ,You, my Beloved , I bleed for You...

❋ LOVE ❋

Can you trap the song of a sparrow

And the morning mist upon the waters?

Will your hands steal them away from the rest of us?

Can the shining of midday be only over your spirit?

And the wetness of the waterfalls?

Can you hide them in your quarters?

Such is the Love in heart,

Blessed be the one that allows the beauty of all to bless us all,

To be spread in abundance as the wind caresses the bosom of prairies,

For God created it,

And it is good, and it is good

Because it is Love.

❀ Condors' Song ❀

I soar like condors high,

Child of the universe in winds of bliss I breathe,

I am here, my gaze is gentle, my awakening never-ending,

I move into the fresh moments of all seasons,

We know each other, off course we do,

For we share the adamantine gem of our Beloved,

And the word is "Love,"

My wings rest, again I am ready,

Let another day begin,

The blessing have but begun,

Pure, pristine, unseen in all that is.

And all is well, and so it is.

🌸 POMEGRANATE 🌸

I'll peel You a pomegranate

I'll offer to You every and each seed

I'll place the joys of this moment upon my lips

And the life of Your Love within my heart

Your sacredness shall become mine

Your fruit, the fruit I'll share with the ones You place in my path

I'll find You in their eyes

We'll enjoy Your pomegranate together

We'll sing praises to Your spirit

And celebrate the abundance of all that You are.

❀ The Kiss ❀

Stone me

Stone me

Stone me sweet brother

Stone me until my very essence is but the mere memory of existence

Stone me until distance is forgotten

Stone me until dust is no longer

Stone me until your tears of doubt become oceans of righteousness

Will you be able to Love me then?

Will you be able to hold your child in your arms and see my eyes in his face?

Will you hold on to your mother's hand, and recognize in her breath my last breath?

Will you use those trees of my crucifixion to make a fire where you'll attempt to burn your guilt?

Yes, I'd rather you stone me,

For denying my Beloved is denying the beauty I see in you,

I am but the mere reflection of yourself,

And also the rock that you punish me with,

Would I consider a kiss in the cheek?

Please, better to stone me.

🏵 GRATITUDE 🏵

Was it only the fears?

Was it the moonlight?

Or the cries of the mother bear over the hard winter?

I heard you my Lord,

And it was in all of it that I found You,

In the salmon in the river,

In the raven up above,

In the olive tree and her fruit,

In the palm of my sweet brother,

Fears and winters,

Tears and wonders,

I am with you,

You keep me warm, safe, loved,

I am grateful.

❀ Reverence ❀

I sage this temple of mine my Beloved, Your temple,

I am blessed in your healing smoke of calm,

I walk the four corners of spirit

And into the longest journey I then descend into my heart,

Your home,

My sweet brother visits me,

He calls you the Christ, I smile at You...

He calls you Allah , I smile at You...

He calls you Great Spirit, I smile at You...

He continues naming you, I continue smiling,

I smudge your space of reverence where I can become one with my sweet brother,

For I embrace him, I am embracing You,

I smile at You,

Your smile remains eternal.

I am the smoke,

I am the breath,

You Are, I Am.

❀ WARRIOR ❀

Lay down your heavy armor, wounded warrior,

And let the scales of fear fall along with it,

Wipe your tears of defeat, and smile into the journey of surrender,

Walk in naked into this palace, brave man,

And may your war be but a fleeting cry of yesterday.

Come, come and allow the One to dress you in garments of hope,

In robes of compassion,

In clothes of humanness,

Yes, sweet brother, the war is over and you've lost,

Only to gain the gifts of heavens,

Weapons and plans turned to caring gestures of love,

Hate and judgment, into mercy and forgiveness.

Welcome, welcome, welcome,

I found myself in the lap of God.

Again…

❀ CREATION ❀

In the unfolding of light,

It is true my sweet brother

That the Almighty created Love to sustain His own Bliss.

So we sit in evenings of winter,

We share the bread of life,

The sounds of divine prayers fall deeper,

The awakening of new dreams and laughter dance brighter,

The memories of tender years, warmer,

Warmer the tears of surrender sweet brother,

An embrace onward,

Departure, a last sip of courage,

Renewed in a toast to the heavens,

We were able to be love in our differences.

And there it is,

So it was,

And shall continue.

Our Beloved is pleased,

For tonight peace became us,

For His Bliss remains.

❀ IN TIMES LIKE THIS ❀

Have you ever wondered at the beauty behind the unseen one my sweet brother,

The loving gentle force that opens your eyes to the new day,

The joyful breath that awakens your senses,

Gives you life, eternal life?

In this moment for every moment is this moment,

Have you ever wondered and wished the same for your distant neighbor?

You know, sweet brother,

The one whose words of love are spoken in a different way,

The one whose majesty of skin shines in a different way

The one whose praise of the Beloved

Is a crescendo of light, making the world sing in a different way.

But his heartbeat ... Just the same...

His breath... Just the same...

Held as baby one day... Just the same...

Tears for the lost... Just the same...

Broken hearted... Just the same...

Kisses of joy ... Just the same...

Promises, dreams, laughter, death, rebirth, meals, work, night, heaven, doubt, LIFE... Just the same...

As your precious self....

So my sweet brother....

Wonder the wonders of Oneness and be one with me...

For I just love you...

Just the same as HE loves me...

❖ FALL ❖

Let me fall back into the arms of nothingness my Lord,

Behold me in your silent embrace,

Sing me lullabies of hope,

Melodies of autumn,

That my sorrow be a dove into your spirit,

That my will be the very end of your river,

Tender petals of fall,

O my Beloved,

I am deaf unto my own song,

Sing me Yours,

Let it be one of no sound,

For no sound in You is but the spheres of the universe serenading me into my breath.

And Your tenderness is the smile in my brother's face.

I believe I just heard Your bell of awakening…

I am here Father…

❄ Blue ❄

In indigo You have blessed me,

And the sages offered their wisdom,

I retrieve again, You see,

For knowledge without experience is a loud scream without a sound ,

And those, I know way too well,

So in Your depth, I search for Your light,

I come upon an ocean where my reflection says that I have always found You.

The seers told me that,

They also told me that from that ocean I would fall in love with Your fire,

I am burning, an indigo flame I'm becoming.

Waters and fire are the making of this child of Yours,

Forever in Love with You.

❄ CHRISTMAS ❄

Born into the fire of men's heart,

Hate or love, He is rebirth.

The calling was distant,

The longing present,

The cries of a mother,

The persistence of a father,

The birth of Love it was,

It is, it shall continue,

In the fire of men's heart,

It shall.

No wonder we have called it

The Silent Night...

Praise be to You my Beloved.

❀ Deliverance ❀

A tear drop

A cry in the wilderness of existence

My spirit recognizes your longing sweet brother,

Like you I have been the barge that has carried the precious Beloved to the other margin,

Only to realize the severity of my actions,

So cry, have a good cry sweet brother,

The solace of relief will bless you when you find out that He was the Captain all along.

🏵 BECOMING 🏵

My Beloved if loving You is being on fire,

Let me burn now on end.

If having You is becoming an ocean,

Let me drown in your waters.

If existing in you is the silence of a standing tree,

Let me become a forest.

If sensing You is whirling in hurricanes,

I'll become Your strongest winds.

When all is done and finished,

Lay me down in your earth,

That I may become the dust that will turn into your breath.

❀ Compassion ❀

In my hands I hide my shameful face,

My humanness once again caught up with me,

I am lost in a desert,

A wanderer of nights in valleys of tears,

O my Beloved , may you forgive your perfectly imperfect fool,

Will You become my oasis?

Will You allow my shame to melt under this desert heat?

Will You sooth me with Your coolness of mercy?

When have You created nights with such fire suns

That blind furiously this sinner?

O, but I know your compassion, and I know that from under this
hell you shall bring forth a heaven into the morning sunrise,

The moon will receive me,

I'll be reborn into your mystical plan,

A fountain of miracles shall crown me again.

Forgive me my Lord.

❀ PHOENIX RISING ❀

Embrace me, nourish me,

Bathe me, love me,

I've become the child,

I am the open seed of vulnerability,

The phoenix rising of youth,

The memory of the lost hopes,

With Your embrace I make quilts to warm your children my Lord,

With Your nourishment I share Your food with Your gentle souls,

With Your cleansing I bring healing into the wounded brethren with Your love,

I Am.

❋ Nakedness ❋

Have you drawn the curtain between us sweet brother?

Will I ever be able to perceive your light again?

Do not let your senses deny my love for you,

Let us be light together,

Let us be divine together,

Let us celebrate our flaws together,

And in the vastness of your heart,

Consider a smile,

Lift that curtain sweet brother,

For I let you see my own nakedness,

That you recognize yourself in it.

✵ SPIRIT ✵

Father,

Mother of Light,

I am broken open to Your dream.

Gentle lullabies cradle me into Your heavens,

I fall upward in the circle of Your four winds,

You've made me spirit,

I abide.

The dust that I'll return to will be the breath of the fulfillment,

How sweet are You, Oh Dreamers,

For creation that is Yours is life that is ours,

I will walk the path, even if blinded,

I will guide the blind, for the Light is Yours to lead,

Then, all shall be an awakened reality,

And it shall be good.

❧ Humanity ❧

I've listened for the thrill of the falling angel,

It was only a water drop.

The silhouette left by sister moon, guarded well the onlookers,

They all came to see the pitied one,

I let them watch.

Another drop has fallen, this one from my Beloved,

I tasted it, it has the flavor of mercy,

I've watched for the coming of the armies of hell,

It was only rain that I saw,

The shadows left by the gone sun hidden well from the judges.

They all came to blame the different one,

And I became one with them.

Another drop, this one from one like me.

I tasted it, it is sweet, it has the flavor of humanity,

I've sensed for all that makes me unspoken,

I felt mankind,

We all danced together,

And the three of us cried tears of joy.

❈ ETERNAL OCEAN ❈

Sail with me to over there sweet brother,

Sail with me into the waters of the deep, where salt is saltier, and wet is wetter ,

Come out of your little boat,

Sail with me to the waters of no returning,

Where drowning is breathing,

And sailing is staying.

Waters that will carve His nameless name with tides of sights,

That will leave wanting the storms for the sunny breezes,

Sail with me sweet brother in this vessel of tears turned to laughter,

Reborn in the same breath that butterfly wings conceive tsunamis,

And with me become the Waters of Life,

For His Ocean his sweet and eternal.

❀ Home ❀

Coast of oceans,

Long lost warrior,

Cast your sorrows into the wind,

Mountains free,

Births of wisdom,

Fly in circles of prayer and sing,

Songs of presence, songs of presence,

For the wars were never won,

And in your tears you cry your enemy,

That you killed within your heart,

Coast of oceans, icy waters

Warm your eyes in distant view,

Come back to honor,

The gift of life given,

Come to honor the light within,

The future is bright as healing bends your knees,

And memories are made of hope,

And in hands raised high you find that home is what you give,

In the smile of who receive,

Welcome home.

Welcome home.

Welcome home.

❈ Archer ❈

You made me an archer,

I hunted for you,

Never killing anyone,

I hunted for the joy of your smile.

In the hunting I was one with you

Until I tried to impress you,

I lost my skill,

I began the killing,

I hunted for myself,

Oh Loving Mother of Truth,

The naked body of a lost hunter

Runs wilder than my prey,

A prey that never existed,

For my prey I've become,

Killing me in every breath that I forgot what You created me for.

I shall die then,

Yes indeed,

I'll be just that you made me to be,

For I long for your smile again,

Within ...again,

And again, I'm an archer.

❦ Honey ❦

Kissing honey, I found myself,

In the sweetness of Your mystery,

The woman, the man, the child,

I became,

The river that ascended, the ocean that died ashore,

I have travelled the seasons of all,

I have met You in my cell,

I have met you in my spaciousness.

Some voice yelled at me from a distance and named me the insane one,

I could only smile,

For, for You, Precious Fire.

I am but sane,

I am kissing honey,

I am kissing honey…

❀ Returning To Nothingness ❀

Returning to nothingness,

Returning to nothingness I am,

In the thunder of your silence I become,

Beacon of light,

Friend of the shadow,

That she may become one with You, with me,

I crawl into the circle of existence to be one with all,

I fall into the waters of above,

I woke up to ending songs of dawn, and the heavens bellow,

I am that to which you called forth,

And so I take the offer of this moment to which You make me your servant.

Returning to nothingness,

The fullness of Your mastery quenched in a simple breath,

The One that moves me towards You,

Complete, silent, aware,

Now and again

'Till end of time,

Time that never existed in the thought that you've dreamed for the coming home of this child of yours,

I am home,

My head in your lap,

I returned my beloved,

To the immensity of abundance,

The whisper of this joyful storm,

In this awakening, I am

Returning to nothingness.

❀ GARDEN OF EDEN ❀

I encountered the desert,

Indeed, I drank from the fountains of sorrow and quenched my thirst in the emptiness of mirages,

I took another step, and quick sands loved me into desperation,

I woke up, the desert flourished into the nakedness of being,

I crossed, survived,

Now I lead others into the gateway of the Garden of Eden.

❀ HOLINESS ❀

In silence, my prayer has freed me,

And my soul is a river of eternal waters,

It is the flowing of life that touches other souls,

And we dance to the divine melody of the presence of God.

I am holy.

❀ Wisdom ❀

Guard your lips and your mind,

Wild horses astray may leave injury along the way,

Be mindful of your speech, carry a gentle word in your heart,

Practice it, and you shall master the wisdom of loving communication.

❀ Betrayal ❀

I was starving...

Their touch on my skin felt like Sunday morning...

And like the seventh day, it was good...

For I did not know any different,

And like twin Judas they betrayed my preciousness,

A gentle flame was taken, my eyes glazed...

Some might name a pebble shame... guilt...embarrassment ...pain,

I was starving, no one offered mercy.

Only forgiveness has set me free.

❀ Childhood ❀

Her silence carved a deeper wound than his hatred,

Father, father, will you stop now?

Mother, mother...

Your eyes were heavier than his sway,

Did you became an extension of God's silence?

Your locked lips burned deeper than offensive words,

Two little gods unleashing their unspoken hurt on the gentler, softer, weaker soul...

I weep.

❀ PERFUME ❀

I wonder if cardamom was the scent of the Buddha,

Or Mohammed's essence was juniper,

Jesus, lavender?

Krishna, cinnamon?

Or did all of these men share the same perfume of our suffering?

Where the drops of sweat tasted like blood,

And the breathing was heavier when a brother has fallen.

Will I claim the unbeauty of the ordinary as the miracle of ages

And take the scents of cruel life as the prophets did?

Yes, yes, I must.

For how can I rejoice in the sunrise if I don't rejoice in the darkest clouds?

❀ Healing ❀

Will I dare to walk the path of fire?

Be consumed in the eternal flame of doubt and still trudge?

Allow the healing of my soul to become the caldron of thought and await the calming of truth?

Indeed I choose it all, for bliss is the journey and much peace abides at the end of each breath.

❀ CANVAS ❀

This experience that is your life,

A magnificent canvas,

What colors will manifest your spirit?...

In what brightness will you reveal your love to your neighbor, your lover, yourself?...

Will you hide in the shades of the shadow, your envy, your anger, your judgment?...

Or will you allow the masterpiece of this art creation that is your life be exposed in all that you are?...

Knowing that in your revealed true self lies the whole essence of Divinity... And Love shall emerge indeed...

Let your breath be the brush that strokes your creativity, and brings your entire beauty into existence...

You shall radiate and embrace your artist within your sacred heart...

And just be.

❀ Humility ❀

Humble me in my silence, Oh sweet Creator...

That I may know myself as You know me...

That I may nurture myself as You nurture me...

That I may love myself as You love me...

So that I may become that beam of light in acceptance of others as You are of me...

So that I may become that ray of hope to others as You are to me...

So that I may become the blessing to others as You are within me...

So that I may continue to celebrate Your magnificence in my utter nothingness...

Shalom...Shalom...Shalom.

❀ KNOWING ❀

You have faced the unbearable.

I know.

You have been through the fire.

I know.

You have drunk the tears of sorrow.

I know.

Your heart is gentle,

Your body celestial,

Your mind joyful,

Your soul eternal.

Please know.

Please know.

Please know.

❈ Uncertain Path ❈

Broken stones in uncertain path,

Flows of rivers never travelled but by your tender mind,

Cloven in heart, bleeding the unseen,

The run for cover under the unprotected sky,

It was always night, wasn't it?

And so one must keep on

For the waters keep on wanting to break the dam.

Oh but how the holding becomes harder,

So many escapes of courage,

But the memorial canvas persisted,

How many more nights to die?

Will the flame appear?

It will, it has.

167

❁ DREAMS ❁

In stardust you held your dreams,

In stars you believed,

All from the depth of your soul, they were taken as lava from a volcano burning it all into nothingness,

As the day emerged, king Sun took them away from your view,

Your stars and dreams all folded in a ray that soon became the yearning whisper of your heart,

"Where?" Your sweet unheard voice spoke.

And with the question you perpetuate your existence,

In endless nights and dying days the hemorrhage of desperation kept your gentle step hoping,

Tears gave a way of becoming years when the heart has refused to open,

How could He?

The only openness He knew came in slashes of suffering,

Was it not, my dreamer?

And it was that feelings became thoughts,

And thoughts prevail as a kingdom,

And as a kingdom thoughts order death onto feelings,

And so the story goes,

The gentle soul hung dreams in stardust,

Dreaming to recognize himself,

But stars and stardust were also taken away in the dream,

And a light prevailed,

Yes,

It does.

❀ CROWN ❀

Crowned child, blessed humanness,

Remember the clouded days of late autumn,

The promises of evening rains and scented warm earth,

How you traveled through those valleys, eyes closed,

Divinity there, right there with you,

And your hiding days in the old cinema,

The walk home, wet feet, cold bones, buried in the fantasies of the scented roasted chestnuts, of others.

Even then you could see God hiding in the corner.

How many lives have you lived that did not belong to you my child?

How many deaths did you endure in silence?

And the bread kneaded by the devil, you broke and made miracles out of sheer hope,

Bless You crowned child,

Your crown is transparent,

Your eyes the eternal longing,

And who will sing your song

When your broken dreams will no longer roll down your lips?

Your beautiful body, shall give a place for a tree,

One that shall bare good fruit,

And remain tall.

Pray, pray that that one dream might not be as the ones forgotten on that big screen in those beginning winter nightmares.

🌸 MASK 🌸

One seating,

One seating only,

The daring remembrance of days

Dare not to allow one's rising.

One seating,

Hand to mouth,

Stiletto topping the world,

Face the invisible enemy, blinded soldier,

Your blood is wanted here where ignorance is paid by religious talk,

Bow, go ahead bow,

Fear,

Fear nothing, and be the cowardly one,

Show not who the real beauty is,

We may not like you,

Too much beauty gets on one's nerves,

And does not go well with all the so-needed death.

Ever consider going fishing?

For when one forgets his humanness the spirit is left, lost somewhere.

❊ Past ❊

Craving the noted wall,

The one blanket of desperation,

Covering the wounded children of past,

The joys of make believe allow for another carving of the soul,

That one will look good over the fireplace during the holidays, my dear.

Wonder about the path, the pierced honesty through your loins,

How alive life feels when men sink their bare hands in mother's soil and scream,

And there's sound to that scream,

There's voice, there's presence,

The child opens her lost sacred heart and mourns her stolen diamond,

The one that would had made her complete,

The scream is loud then,

Trees, and sparrows, vines and rivers scream with him,

The blanket has covered their lost innocence for so long,

Many have felt it, few have expressed it,

And so it goes, so many carvings, above so many fireplaces,

Let them burn, let them burn,

We all keep pretending as we all did before,

Nothing is there.

Kill the child again, craving the place of no belonging,

Craving the noted wall.

❀ Father ❀

Spread your wings with inward sight,

The moonlight of samsara holds your gaze like dripping crystals in dreamland views,

Your nakedness, that of the chandelier imitation let's your illusion fuse into your breath,

You've curled your body into the natal calling,

Your flight is suspended in my nostalgic memories,

Un-dance your step, keep the broken nails of sorrow in that God box where promises were made ashes,

And you drank them in chalices of doom,

Precious child recoil your feathers,

The night is here, you look too tired for another war,

Claim your place in emptiness,

And sleep, sleep the wonders of tomorrow.

❀ SMILE ❀

I call the endless shadow

I remain as silent as the unheard wave

The one that was missed in God's sleeplessness

I trusted the walk

And the fog as dense as the soul offered to be my guide

I remain as silent as the unfelt sorrow

The one that was denied in God's numbness

I trusted the shadow

And as dark as itself it brought the mirror closer than my skin

I saw the reflection of my nothingness

And the Beloved smiled,

And I smiled with Him.

❀ GARDEN ❀

On the path to the garden of Eden,

Remaining aware of life as life,

Illusion comes in smoky lights and the mind loses the focus.

To what garden are you walking?

Is the word stronger or the silence?

Aloneness shall bear the fruits of wisdom and freedom,

Eyes open in perpetual prayer.

An awakened prayer of loving action,

Trudging step by step,

Arriving to Eden at this very moment...again.

❀ I BECOME ❀

Calm is the voice of this silence,

I become,

The unraveling of the truth bursts into flames,

The mighty waters of solace submerged the illusion,

I become,

In awe to the ultimate surrender,

The soul graces awareness while the mind attempts a last escape,

Terror seems to emerge,

Not to worry ... The calm voice whispers,

I become, I become, I become,

Awake to the breath,

All else shall continue the alchemy that it offers.

❀ Machines ❀

Surely a pity if the pear tries to become an orange,

Surely sad if a eagle believes herself to be a hen,

Rivers of tears shared in rain when God sees His children forgetting their holiness and becoming machines.

❀ THIS TWO SHALL PASS ❀

Preciousness abides in the silent gift of breath,

The sacred heart unfolding in the morning glory,

As the soul gives joy to the love of the father of Light,

Memories become clouds in the distant indigo sky,

Suffering is the blessed friend now that it's becoming observed,

This too shall pass, as the breath becomes my guide.

❀ Peacefulness ❀

Try and grab the wind,

And you shall grow tired and fall.

Try and hold on to water,

And you shall grow weak and drown.

Let it be and flow in their mystery,

And you shall become and grow wise and calm.

And in their flowing path you shall arrive deep within your awakening.

❊ BEING ❊

You called me wise

But I am only human

You called me successful

But I am only human

You called me a poet

But I am only human

You called me a fool

But I am only human

You called me ignorant

But I am only human

You called me stupid

But I am only human

A precious child of God?

Yes, in my humanness

That I am.

❋ LAMP ❋

The lamp refuses her light to no one,

You've gained my attention.

The rose refuses her fragrance to no one,

You've gained my heart.

The oak three refuses her shade to no one,

You've gained my body.

The rain refuses her coolness to no one,

You've gained my soul.

The air refuses her sweetness to no one,

You've gained my life.

So I breathe You,

I've gained You,

I've gained Your Divine Love.

❋ DIVINE SOUND ❋

Is it a sound?

Is it a whisper?

Is it a voice?

The manifestation of thunder?

The softness of a gentle breeze?

The crumbling of fallen boulders?

Is it the song of a sparrow?

The cradling of a river bank?

The orchestra of a forest adagio?

Is that you my Beloved?

Is that You?

I can hear your sweetness,

I keep listening to silence.

❀ Depth ❀

Crash Your waves against my body, crash them.

Embrace me with Your higher tides.

I'll become Your grains of sand,

In the infinite shore of Your gentle caring.

Leave the mark of Your presence over and within,

Make me part of Your unspoken mystery,

Roll me back into Your deep waters,

As they roll down my face in smaller drops,

In my eyes they are witnesses,

I have seen through my blindness,

I have tasted the salt of You.

Submerge me,

Floating is but a painful tease to this servant of yours.

❀ LORD OF LIGHT ❀

Oh Lord of Light,

Love and tenderness you are,

How sweet your embrace to this beggar of truth,

My heart is laced in passion,

But You want me as a child,

My mind is poisoned by arrogance,

You asked me to be a fool,

I'm a drunkard that can't get enough of Your wine,

But You keep me as sober as the ocean.

I stumble into this cell of mine and find myself at Your feet,

Let me wash them with my tears of joy.

I'll stay awake,

I'll stay awake,

I'll stay awake.

❁ SINNER ❁

You have called me wise,

I thank you.

But I'm nothing but a sinner seeking God's heart.

And I fail, and fall, and fall again.

I shall continue getting up to be in your wisdom sweet brother.

❉ WAKE UP ❉

I heard the gongs of life,

They yelled

"Wake up, wake up,

Get out of your dormant slumber,

Run into life,

Awake."

Bright is the light that awakens this spirit,

From the boundless love of God

I gain the courage to become.

I'm more than my mere thoughts,

The mind has begun to serve the heart.

It hurts, it is good, and so it is.

Awake.

❀ POISON ❀

Yes, I have heard your words

My heart has sought refuge in silence for fear of illness,

Speak of your trudging,

Speak of your suffering,

Of the joys and sorrows of your destiny,

Sweet brother, yield to words from the lives of others,

For such is poison, that neither your precious heart can take,

And mine can't bear,

But mostly, it saddens the very essence of our loving Creator.

❋ BREAKING BREAD ❋

Fret not about the beginning or the end of it all, sweet brother,

For all is here, was and shall remain.

Allow the mystery to unfold in your smile,

And let it become mine.

Let us then break bread on this very fine day and share stories of the heart.

You and I, fully present, the three of us.

❁ Gems ❁

Indeed the gems are boundless

In this atrium of silence

I gathered them all, one by one

I place them in order

And You come and take them all,

Throw them away,

Misplace them, hide them

And I come back again

Again I sit with You,

That's how much you love me.

❋ THE SERVANT ❋

Not from your head but from your heart, sweet brother,

Allow your mind to humble itself to your heart,

Be in the sacredness of its silence,

Often and always seek its council,

And surrender to its guidance.

In your head you claim your will,

Your rights, your plans, your all,

In your heart you'll claim the will of the Living One,

His compassion, His Love, His forgiveness,

Let your mind serve your heart, sweet brother.

❀ Remaining ❀

Remain awake,

That's right, the voyage you so desire is long but short,

The knowledge you so long for is so faraway yet so near,

The peacefulness that you seek seems so distant yet lives within you,

So, remain awake.

Remain in here, there where you are,

Learn from yourself, there in your inner wisdom,

And in your sweet silence become the gentle soul that is your true essence,

Remain awake, remain enlightened.

❀ FIRE ❀

If Your love were a river,

I would be a leaf floating about into Your ocean.

If Your love were the wind,

I would be the feather drifting into other lands.

But it's fire my Lord, it's fire,

And so I'll be a gentle flame burning with Your existence within me.

❧ Lament ❧

In my lament I left the famine and embraced the vastness of You,

In the remembrance of my sacred heart I found the Divine You,

No longer shall I hunger

For your supply is everlasting,

No longer shall I thirst

For your well is abundant,

My lament has become our embrace,

Even my garments shed the scent of your presence.

How blessed You have made me.

❀ TIDES ❀

The thousand tides that I watched fade,

They faithfully returned,

And so my breath flows to You my Lord,

And to me You return.

Shalom, shalom, shalom.

❀ GIFTS ❀

I craved the moon

Received a world

I craved a world

Was blessed with his nothingness

I offer both

And I gained all

I gained all.

❁ CHANGING ❁

I wanted to change the multitudes,

"Change that stone."

I heard.

I wanted to change the ones around me,

"Change that stone."

I heard.

I want to change myself,

"You shall transform your stone to a diamond."

I heard.

❋ Subtleness ❋

Indeed, sweet brother,

Becoming like the wolf will bring great wisdom.

Indeed, sweet brother,

Reading all the divine books will bring great knowledge.

Indeed, sweet brother, your suggestions have the weight of value.

Your sweet answers have overlooked the subtleness of humanness

And the joys and sorrows of the path.

Change must happen, indeed,

Within one's self.

Please show me, don't tell me.

❋ KNOW THYSELF ❋

The silence spoke,

You can never go home sweet one,

My heart sank,

The tears streamed,

The longing, oh the longing,

The cry that is lost in time,

I can never go home.

But I did, and home was not there,

So the silence speaks again.

Now, there you are,

Here you are,

And wherever you are

In the sacredness of your heart,

You are home.

But I want to go back,

And the silence insists

That back is not home, sweet one,

You can't ever go back.

Rejoice in the breath and just be

Just be and it will be enough.

Still... I cry...I long ...

Home is where you are my dear one,

The silence speaks again.

Know thyself within thyself,

And you are home, so....

Welcome Home.

Welcome Home.

Welcome Home.

www.ingramcontent.com/pod-product-compliance
Lightning Source LLC
Chambersburg PA
CBHW030011110426
42741CB00032B/273